Professional Studies/ Psychiatric Technician

BECAUSE IT'S WRONG
BULLIES VS. NAZIS

Professional Studies/ Psychiatric Technician

BECAUSE IT'S WRONG
BULLIES VS. NAZIS

LYDIA GREICO M.A.

ReadersMagnet, LLC

Because It's Wrong: Bullies Vs. Nazis
Copyright © 2019 by Lydia Greico M.A.

Published in the United States of America
ISBN Paperback: 978-1-950947-50-8
ISBN eBook: 978-1-950947-51-5

All rights reserved. No part of this publication may be reproduced, stored in a retrieval system or transmitted in any way by any means, electronic, mechanical, photocopy, recording or otherwise without the prior permission of the author except as provided by USA copyright law.

The opinions expressed by the author are not necessarily those of ReadersMagnet, LLC.

ReadersMagnet, LLC
10620 Treena Street, Suite 230 | San Diego, California, 92131 USA
1.619. 354. 2643 | www.readersmagnet.com

Book design copyright © 2019 by ReadersMagnet, LLC. All rights reserved.
Cover design by Ericka Walker
Interior design by Shemaryl Evans

In memory

For my brother Joseph and my mother Gloria.
May they rest in peace.

Contents

Dedication ix
Acknowledgements xi
Forward xiii
Preface xvii

Chapter 1: What is Bullying 1
Chapter 2: Who Was the Biggest Bully of all Time? 19
Chapter 3: Bullying in WWII 32
Chapter 4: Dachau Concentration Camp 44
Chapter 5: Dachau Subcamps 55
Chapter 6: The Liberation of Dachau 63
Chapter 7: Sobibor 72
Chapter 8: Treblinka 80
Chapter 9: Auschwitcz-Birkenau 87
Chapter 10: Buchenwald 103
Chapter 11: Manzanar 110
Chapter 12: Why did I write about bullying
            first then do the concentration
            camps second? 119

Chapter 13: A Comparison and A Contrast
    Bullies VS. Nazis 127

Final thoughts 131
References 133

Dedication

I am dedicating this book to all the victims of bullying as far back in history and as it is happening today; People in the workplace getting bullied in America, our children in schools, and family life. I am also including the Jews that died in the holocaust in such a horrific manner with reckless disregard for life by the Nazis.

Acknowledgements

First I would like to say that without God this book would have not been possible. I believe that through him all things are possible. So to God be the glory! He gave me the power and strength and gifts to write this book. Next I want to thank my family and my extended family for giving me the space to do what I had to do in creating this book; For understanding my efforts in doing the research and for understanding why I had to miss family functions yet again to meet all my personal deadlines. I want to thank Sally Harrington, a former collegue, for giving me her notes on bullying from the ACTE conference. Next I would like to thank Rabbi Hiam Asa for his input and guidance. He now deceased was a survivor of Treblinka and I am honored to know him and his wife. When Rabbi Asa died my pastor Father Gilberto Escobedo took his place and he sat with me and counseled me when things got so painful I had to put the book aside for a while. I would like to thank Carrae Ettestad whose father was in WWII as a POW, rode to Dresden in a boxcar, and was also incarcerated there. I interviewed her dad when he was alive and remember his stories of being a POW. Next and the biggest thank you goes to both the AICE The **American-Israeli Cooperative Enterprise** (AICE) was established in 1993 as a nonprofit and nonpartisan organization to strengthen the U.S.-Israel relationship by emphasizing the fundamentals of the alliance and-the values our nations share They said I didn't have to cite anything I retrieved on their page but of course I will. And the American Medical Association (AMA) I want to thank Dr Ron Raya for helping me edit the book chapter by chapter and for helping me with the APA standards...and support. I would also like to thank my spiritual guide who helped me after Rabbi Asa died. His name is Reverand Gilberto Escobedo, I would also like to thank Netflix for letting me view their documentaries, old news reels and movies depicting what really went on in all the bullying. They said to use them as long as I needed too. For that I am grateful because I want this book to be fact not here say.

Forward

What the author reveals in her book, I personally experienced for over thirteen years in my young life. It happened at school, at church, with my neighborhood friends, and sometimes even my family joined the ranks.

The details of the experience are not important; it is the *outcome* which is. Forty nine years afterwards, the scars will never be erased. However, I've used my experience in doing a better job in my career, in my human services volunteering and deeply understand others' pain which offer comfort to others, more sensitivity to those I work with and deeper insight into the lives I touch in volunteering.

The scars of humiliation have left me a more humble person. The scars of others laughing at me have resulted in little self esteem, no positive self image and low self confidence. I think the worst of what is left from the bullying experience is that I was robbed of learning adequate socialization skills like others in my age group who were growing up, too. To this day, I continually miss social cues that I know little about, but others assume I *should*. This often leads to avoidable misunderstandings. I have to try harder to be a "normal" person who has had none of my experiences. I choose to overcome this deep pain in how I express myself in the world I live in.

I'm effective at looking "outside the box," because I lived outside of it in my formative years. I'm effective at advocating for those who need defending because I've experienced what it is like to be defenseless. I'm effective at being an oddball because; after all, I am. I'm effective at drawing others outside of their own self concept to show them they have value, even though they find it unbelievable. I'm effective at follow up because of being forgotten. I'm effective at encouraging others because I know what it is like to be discouraged. If I laugh at myself, others can approach me even if I am a "half a bubble off."

The effect of bullying has left me to become a more genuine person who has the courage of my convictions. The strength that it takes to endure bullying has led to having the strength to stand and speak, "*the emperor wears no clothes.*" Finally, being misunderstood has led me to love more deeply and use a wealth of understanding to attempt to solve the challenges I face each day. All of my life, I have drawn closer to God, which has facilitated a remarkable spiritual journey. None of this transformation would have been possible without depending upon Him. I owe my tormentors nothing, but I owe my Lord all in making it possible to turn bad into good and righting many wrongs.

Cynthia R. McCue, M.A.
Orange County, CA

Preface

What is a bully? Who gets bullied?, What is a scapegoat?, Why do people get bullied?, How far back does bullying back go in history?, What were the worst cases of bullying in history? These are the questions I will answer in my book entitled STOP BULLYING BECAUSE IT'S WRONG. I decided to do this book because bullying seems to be the way of life these days. Bullying occurs In schools, sometimes in family life, in the jails, prisons, in employment; virtually everywhere. People who have been on the job for a long time retire long before their time because they just can't stand being bullied anymore. They are sick of all the empty threats by management and peers while they are trying to do the right thing. When will this end? When will people begin to say "I've had enough and it has to stop"? How can we improve things in America with bullying on such a rampage?

Jesus was bullied; Jews in the Holocaust were bullied and took the hardest known blows in history known today in religious worlds. The American Indians were bullied off their land and on to reservations, Kids in school today are bullied; celebrities kids; people who are different are bullied. The Japanese got bullied in 1942. We had our own holocaust. There is no end to bullying in this country and in this book I want to talk about all of the reasons for bullying. I will go into deep depth showing incidents of bullying. Why do humans keep trying to find a way to hurt one another? Isn't one of Gods commandments to love your neighbor as yourself?

What possesses us to hurt one another and derive pleasure from hurting another? Could it be because we live in a Godless society and we are reaping what we have sown? Does the devil have such a reign on our country now?

We all have a free will and not everyone sees life as a sacred gift from God that it is. I will discuss who gets bullied, why and possible solutions. It has to be said and now especially when bullying is on such a rampage. Everywhere we look especially in the school system, and in life activities there is bullying. The saying goes that history repeats itself and it is. Bullying was such a problem in New York that a bill was passed against it. Why must man continuously try to hurt one another? One can only pass it off as free will for a while but not for ever.

Bullying started as far back as Jesus days. Look at the way he was put to death. Pilot picked the worst most societal devastating way to kill Jesus; crucifixion. He was whipped, beaten, spit on, hair pulled from his beard from the very people of he had chosen and elevated……..His own race. One week they were praising him and the next week they crucified him. How could this be? This was bullying to the nth degree. This is what this book BECAUSE IT'S WRONG" is essentially about.

2 Thessalonians 2:3 Let no man deceive you by any means: for that day shall not come, except there come a falling away first, and that man of sin be revealed the son of perdition;

Invictus

Out of the night that covers me,
Black as the Pit from pole to pole,
I thank whatever gods may be
For my unconquerable soul.

In the fell clutch of circumstance
I have not winced nor cried aloud.
Under the bludgeonings of chance
My head is bloody, but unbowed.

Beyond this place of wrath and tears
Looms but the Horror of the shade,
And yet the menace of the years
Finds, and shall find, me unafraid.

It matters not how strait the gate,
How charged with punishments the scroll.
I am the master of my fate:
I am the captain of my soul.

William Earnest Henley

Chapter 1

What is Bullying

The word bully comes from Germany but it was spelled Boulle and it referred to a girlfriend. It was a man's girlfriend and over the years it has evolved into what it is today. Bullying is an imbalance of power and a form of overly aggressive behavior. Bullying is detrimental to a person's well-being and development. It can include verbal harassment, physical assault or coercion and may be directed repeatedly towards particular victims, perhaps on grounds of race, religion, gender, sexuality, or ability. The "imbalance of power" may be social power and/or physical power. The victim of bullying is sometimes referred to as a "target" or a "scapegoat". Dr. Dan Olweus, in Norway, did the ground-breaking research on bullying from 1975 to the present. His work is the foundation of all current bullying prevention interventions. (Stop Bullying Now,2013) He began with a review of research on how youth become aggressive. Teens do not have a mature grasp on the finality of death. To teens with low self esteem and poor self image, being bullied is devastating to them. This is not preventing teen suicide. Bullying mixed with low self esteem is an incentive to commit suicide. Over 6000 high school young adults have taken their own lives due to bullying.

Why stop bullying?

Bullies are five times as likely to become adult criminals as non-bullies. Targets of bullying are more likely to be depressed as adults. Preventing bullying lowers rates of vandalism, fighting, theft and truancy. Preventing bullying improves school climate.

According to the AMA of Scientific affairs, bullying is a negative behavior that involves a pattern of repeated aggression; deliberate intent to harm or disturb a victim despite apparent victim distress and a real or perceived imbalance of power; with the more powerful child, persons or groups attacking a physically or psychologically vulnerable victim. There are 4 basic forms of bullying. There are physical attacks involving bodily harm or destruction of property. There are verbal attacks seeking to damage self-esteem through name calling and teasing. There are rational attacks that persuade others to reject or exclude the victim. What has happened to this country? Now there is cyber bullying too. Social media programs are notorious for teens bullying teens as well as cellphone bullying. This is ridiculous. How many ways can we hurt one another.

According to an AMA report 10% of school children are bullied regularly by a classmate. One half of all school children are bullied at some time during their years of education. Adults often dismiss bulling as "kids being kids" but it is a serious health problem that can have long-term effects on a victim's psychological well being. Physicians are calling parents and school officials to work together to identify students who are bullies or who are being bullied. Seven to fifteen percent of school children are considered bullies and they share common personality traits. Most have been the victims of physical abuse or bullying themselves usually at home. Bullies are aggressive, controlling and dominating with an over inflated self-image, and often have difficulty empathizing with others. Boys, girls, men and women and teachers can be bullies. Victims of bullying are introverted, passive and easily intimidated. Sometimes classmates perceive them as "different" in some way such as race, ethnicity, sexual orientation, exceptional academic ability, or even a haircut or clothing style. In two thirds of the school shootings over the past few years the shooters were carrying out revenge on bullies. As a result of these tragedies researchers are turning their attention to bullying and we are beginning to understand its consequences. Victims of bullying may exhibit symptoms such as sleep disturbances, bed wetting, abdominal pain, and headaches. In addition to cuts, bruises and other injuries that could be inflicted by physical confrontations. Adolescent victims of bullying may resort to alcohol or drug abuse and some may even be considering suicide according to the report. Adults can also turn to alcohol or drugs or even suicide from being bullied. Research suggests that teachers see about fifty percent of bullying incidents but only thirty six per cent of those incidents are addressed. What are we teaching our children? How come they know so much about bullying????? Why can't we all live in harmony and peace. Teachers your only job isn't to teach; it's to protect students and you are all designated reporters. Report students or discipline them.

Suggestions in Helping Victims of Bullying

Ask your students, or co workers to confidentially identify three individuals whom they think most need a friend. Compile a highly confidential list of the ones who are named. Solicit the help of teachers in the school system or management in the workplace, to take subtle steps to help these children and or adults succeed in the social arena. Another suggestion would be to assign the victims of bullying to a "buddy". The buddy system is an excellent example one of the best protections against bullying.

Have your teachers and supervisors brainstorm about "how they can throw some really positive things in the victims' way." Pair socially isolated individuals with potential friends. Arrange as much as you can without being pushy. Recognize that bullying in schools is under-reported for several reasons. Some children do not want to tell an authority figure because they are afraid the bully will retaliate with greater force. Tell victims to document everything that happens to them. Others are discouraged by adults' dismissive reactions. The most important thing an adult can do about bullying is to address it. Say; "we don't do that here" or give the bully a signal that you recognize his behavior as bullying. By not addressing it you are sending a signal that the behavior is okay. Suggestions for parents in dealing with victims are to Watch out for signs of bullying. The symptoms of victims of bullying include avoidance of certain people or situations, sudden changes in behavior or academic performance, injuries, damaged self image or threats of suicide. It is essential that you believe your child/ co-worker about being bullied. When discussing bullying ask questions, listen and respond with caring and reassurance. Talk to your child's teacher and school principal, or management and ask them to investigate the bullying complaint. Remember that bullying and confrontations with bullies usually occur in unsupervised or under supervised areas such as hallways, bathrooms, locker rooms, employee lounges, school buses, and playgrounds. Increased supervision may alleviate the problem. Teach your child/ co-worker how to be assertive and seek help from someone in authority immediately, when confronted by a bully. Role-play situations and rehearse responses to teasing to help children/co-workers feel more confident. Tell whomever it is to simply walk away when possible. Encourage your child to join sports teams, music groups or extracurricular clubs according to his or her interests. Involvement in these activities builds self confidence and self respect by sharpening social skills and allowing children to develop new abilities. Make sure your co-worker has a friend. The reason being; because two friends are less likely to be bullied.

What Should You Do if You Think Your Child/co-worker is a Bully?

Talk to your child's teacher or school administrator or school counselor if they are not aware of this behavior. They can monitor your child at school and alert you about any discipline problems. Seek the help of a mental health professional if your child's aggressive behavior continues. A pediatrician or family physician can provide a referral to a counselor, child psychiatrist or someone to help you learn strategies for dealing with his or her behavior. If you cannot afford a Psychiatrist your child's school can set you up with a social worker. Parents, teachers and management are the first line of defense for identifying and preventing bullying and physicians are available to help you. The earlier we can identify an individual who is a bully or who is being bullied the better chance there is of stopping the behavior. The easiest way to understand bullying is through looking at these analogies: Spouse abuse, Sexual harassment. All involve imbalance of power. In all these forms of abuse the perpetrator blames the victim for the abuse. In all three the victim may blame him or herself for the abuse, if it is not stopped. How has society reacted to abuse? Through denial *"It's not important;" "He didn't mean it."* By blaming the victim or asking the victim to solve the problem: *"You should wear different clothes;" "Just GET the dinner on the table on time;" "He just does it because he knows it bothers you."* Through comprehensive intervention including training, consequences, and helping abusers change, positive peer pressure, and support for targets.

Lydia Greico M.A.

When Teachers Bully Students

The dunce cap, standing in the corner, having one hand whacked with a ruler, having one' poor grade announced to the class: all these methods that at one time were a common occurrence in educational settings might now fall under the category of bullying teachers. Bullying teachers can act by using degrading words and treatment, as well as physical punishments, swearing at the students, and getting physical with them. Other school employees besides teachers can bully students, including coaches, custodians, security personnel, and the front office staff, even the principal. The public display of a bullying victim's inadequacy often has a different feel in the classroom in which most work is independent and grades can be returned privately versus in the gym, on the sports field, or in the shop setting, in which nearly all work is on display, making everyone aware of the victim's situation. The teacher responding to a student while standing beside his or her desk can maintain some semblances of privacy; the coach or teacher responding to a student half a football field or gymnasium away will likely be heard by all. Thus, in some school settings, humiliation is more likely for a sensitive student, even when correction or constructive criticism is given, let alone when teacher bullying occurs.

It is unclear whether teacher bullying may actually set the stage for peer bullying.

Teacher bullying may go unreported for several reasons. The victim may not trust the system to support or believe him or her, especially if there are any instances in which the victim had infringed school behavior rules. The victim may also fear retribution by the teacher in the form of a lowered grade or more teacher bullying behavior. The victim may also fear retribution by students who are in good standing with the teacher. When teachers bully an entire class, the feeling may be that they have the support of the school and that everyone must know and accept this behavior. Teachers may also bully other teachers and school staff.

How children become aggressive:

According to Dr Dan Olweas of Norway, Bullies often come from homes where there is little warmth and adult attention. In these homes, adults discipline inconsistently, using angry, emotional outbursts and physical discipline. Olweus built his bullying prevention intervention by creating school and family environments that *changed* the patterns that create aggression.

Lydia Greico M.A.

Effective Bullying Prevention

The program strives to develop a school (and ideally a home) environment characterized by: warmth, positive interest, and involvement by adults; firm limits to unacceptable behavior; non-hostile, nonphysical negative consequences consistently applied in cases of ...unacceptable behaviors; and where adults act as authorities and positive role models." Counseling aggressive youth (Olweus,Limber 1999).

The program " Stop Bullying Now" headed by Stan Davis helps students think about these questions after they know what their consequences are:

- What did you do?

- What was wrong with that?

- What problem were you trying to solve?

- Activating bystanders.

- How will you solve that problem next time?

As individuals reflect on their behavior they learn how their behavior affects others and find different ways to meet their needs. Stop Bullying Now encourages individuals to Speak up to bullies, Ask adults or management for help, And reach out as friends to isolated peers.

- "Where, after all, do universal human rights begin? In small places, close to home,-so close and so small that they cannot be seen on any maps of the world. Yet they are the world of the individual person; the neighborhood he lives in; the school or college she attends; the factory, farm, or office where he works. Such are the places where every man, woman, and child seeks equal justice, equal opportunity, equal dignity without discrimination. Unless these rights have meaning there, they have little meaning anywhere. Without concerted citizen action to uphold them close to home, we shall look in vain for progress in the larger world."

—Eleanor Roosevelt

Parents, how do you know the schools your children attend are free from bullying? Supervisors, how do you know that your places of employment are free from bullying? Isn't it time to get involved? If you nip it in the beginning and stop it in its tracks before the individual keeps this up so maybe there won't be so much going on. Schools and workforces across the nation have bullying policies in place and they are working. Let's all get them in our schools and workforce so our individuals won't have to grow up in such a hateful environment. It's hard enough to be a teenager or a young adult; why compound their problems and add bullying to their lives. People shouldn't be pushed out of their jobs because of bullying and retaliation.

Bullying isn't just going on in the schools. It also goes on in the workforce. People at work can't stand it and wind up retiring early, because supervisors choose to turn the other cheek and ignore the bullying of their staff. They should be made to withstand some and see what it does to those being bullied. It happens all the time in the workforce. People just pass it off as someone is having a bad day but when the person seems to be having a bad day every day there should be a stop to it. Many times a workforce bully will target another person who they see as weak when actually that person is just trying to get by doing their job.

What has this got to do with Workplace Bullying?

Bullying situations have been described as "mini-holocausts." This is not meant to insult survivors and family members of those lost in the Holocaust. Death is death. However, many bullied Targets feel as though they have been imprisoned by cruel tyrants, too. Many of the group dynamics mirror the relationship between Nazis and the locals in the invading countries. Bullying leads to terrorization to instill fear, to subjugate people, and tyrants are inevitably outnumbered by normal, peace-loving people, the task seems impossible without help. Collaborators overestimate safety of siding with the tyrant (all are eventually hurt) and victims cannot understand the betrayal of colleagues tyrants divide the group, pitting colleagues against each other. Displays of courage and a refusal to give in to fear can successfully stop the tyrants government administrators fell under the influence of the tyrants, sealing the victims' fate.

Stifling the tyrant requires a simple ethical principle— to do the right thing on behalf of a fellow human being, regardless of whom they are, what they wear or where they choose to be employed. Remember there is no way to make a wrong action right.

NOTE PAGE

NOTE PAGE

NOTE PAGE

NOTE PAGE

NOTE PAGE

Chapter 2

Who Was the Biggest Bully of all Time?

Who really was Hitler? To say he was a monster would be preposterous but to say his actions were that of a monster would be correct. He was, in this writers opinion and lifetime, the biggest bully of all time. He grew up in a normal Catholic family although, his grandfather was Jewish. Of course this was one of his biggest secrets. Born to parents Alois Hitler Sr. 1837-1903, He was the illegitimate child of Ana Maria Schicklgruber. In 1876 Hitler's father was baptized Catholic but his father, Hitler's grandfather was Jewish. Hitler's hatred of the Jews started when he was rejected by the Art school where he wanted to attend. The rest is history and already mentioned in prior chapters.

Lydia Greico M.A.

HITLER'S GROWING UP YEARS

According to Hitler's sister Paula ""Adolf challenged my father to extreme harshness and got his sound thrashing every day. He was a scrubby little rogue, and all attempts of his father to thrash him for his rudeness and to cause him to love the profession of an official of the state were in vain. How often on the other hand did my mother caress him and try to obtain with her kindness where the father could not succeed with harshness". ..." Adolf Hitler's only boyhood friend, August Kubizek, recalled Hitler as a shy, reticent young man, yet he was able to burst into hysterical fits of anger towards those who disagreed with him. The two became inseparable during these early years and Kubizek turned out to be a patient listener.

Kubizek, then sixteen, first met Adolf Hitler, fifteen, late in 1904 when both were competing for standing room at the opera. He was a good audience for Hitler, who often rambled for hours about his hopes and dreams. Sometimes Hitler even gave speeches complete with wild hand gestures to his audience of one. Hitler would only tolerate approval from his friend and could not stand to be corrected, a personality trait he had shown in high school and as a younger boy as well. Then one day in 1905 the pair went to see a performance of Wagner's *Rienzi* at the Linz Memorial Theater. This became a decisive event for the teenaged Hitler, as he was to refer to it after he came to power. In Kubizek's biography of Hitler *The Young Hitler I Knew, 1953*, he recalls how it had a terrifying impact upon Hitler, who left the theater in a state of trance:

> "Adolf stood in front of me; and now he gripped both my hands and held them tight. He had never made such a gesture before. I felt from the grasp of his hands how deeply moved he was. His eyes were feverish with excitement. Never before and never again have I heard Adolf Hitler speak as he did in that hour, as we stood there alone under the stars, as though we were the only creatures in the world. He now spoke of a mission that he was one day to receive from our people, in order to guide them out of slavery, to the heights of freedom"...

So what changed his mind? Apparently at one time he was a decent person. What caused his deep hatred of the Jewish race enough for him to want to practice genocide?

Thirty years later, the boyhood friends would meet again in Bayreuth, and Kubizek told Adolf Hitler what he remembered of that night, assuming that the enormous multitude of impressions and events which had filled these past decades would have pushed into the background the experience of a seventeen year old youth. But after a few words Kubizek sensed that Hitler vividly recalled that hour and had retained all its details in his memory. Hitler's words were unforgettable for August Kubizek.

Some years later in his military life, Adolf Hitler already showed traits that characterized his later life: inability to establish ordinary human relationships, intolerance and hatred of especially the Jews, a tendency toward denunciatory outbursts, readiness to live in a fantasy-world and so to escape his failure.

He learned to loathe brilliant, charming, cosmopolitan Vienna for what he called its Semitism. More to his liking was homogeneous Munich, his real home after 1913. To this man of no trade and few interests World War I was a welcome event which gave him some purpose in life.

So Hitler went to Munich, Germany and when World War I began in 1914, he volunteered for service in the German army. Hitler was twice decorated for bravery, but only rose to the rank of corporal. When World War I ended Hitler was in a hospital recovering from temporary blindness possibly caused by a poison gas attack. In 1930, a worldwide depression hit Germany and Hitler promised to rid Germany of Jews and Communists and to reunite the German speaking part of Europe. In July, 1932, the Nazis received about 40% of the vote and became the strongest party in Germany. On January 30,1933, President Paul von Hindenburg appointed Hitler Chancellor of Germany. Once in this position, Hitler moved quickly toward attaining a dictatorship. When von Hindenburg died in 1934, Hitler already had control of Germany. After Hitler came to power, sales of *Mein Kampf* skyrocketed, making him a rich man. In Germany, where newlyweds received a copy of the book from the government, 6 million copies had been issued by 1940, and by 1942, Hitler himself boasted that *Mein Kampf* had the largest sales of any book in the world – apart from the Bible. By one estimate, Hitler received $1 million a year in royalty payments alone.

Adolf Hitler's war with the Jews now stepped up in pace. Whereas before, anti-Semitic rhetoric helped the Nazis get elected, now they had the power to put some of their ideas into action. In April 1933, Jews were banished from government jobs, a quota was established banning Jews from university, and a boycott of Jewish shops enacted.

In 1935, the infamous Nuremberg Laws were passed. These classed Jews as German "subjects" instead of citizens. Intermarriage was outlawed, more professions were closed to Jews, shops displayed signs reading, "No Jews Allowed." Harassment was common. This started

Hitler's rise to power, and his idea of genocide came into play. All his life Adolf Hitler was seized by an obsession with the Jews and he had always been straightforward about his plans. His dream of a racially "pure" empire would tolerate no Jews and he announced at many occasions the "annihilation of the Jews" living in the territory und In Hitler's mind, murdering millions of Jews could only be accomplished under the confusion of war –from the beginning he was planning a war that would engulf Europe.

Hitler's very first political statement, his letter to Adolf Gemlich on 16 September 1919, already includes a clear declaration of his anti-Semitic position: "Rational anti-Semitism on the other hand, must lead to a systematic legal opposition and elimination of the special privileges that Jews hold, in contrast to the other aliens living among us (alien's legislation). Its final objective must unswervingly be the removal of Jews. In those early days he often spoke of how he would deal with the Jews." *Ausrottung* (extirpation), His favorite *Vernichtung,* (annihilation), *Entfernung* (removal), *Aufräumung* (cleaningup)". Thus according to a police report of a NSDAP meeting on 6 April 1920 he declared:".

> "we have no intention of being emotional anti-Semites who want to create the atmosphere of a pogrom. Instead, our hearts are filled with an

inexorable determination to attack the evil at its roots and to extirpate it root and branch. In order to reach our goal every means will be justified, even if we have to make a pact with the devil."

And that he did. He made a pact with the devil and this is how the holocaust began.

Hitler, at this point became the biggest bully in all of history. On 21 January 1939 Adolf Hitler told the Czech Foreign Minister Chvalkovsky: "We are going to destroy the Jews... The day of reckoning has come."

Matthew 10:28 And fear not them which kill the body, but are not able to kill the soul: but rather fear him which is able to destroy both soul and body in hell.

John 16:2 They shall put you out of the synagogues: yea, the time cometh, that whosoever killeth you will think that he doeth God service.

Matthew 24:9 Then shall they deliver you up to be afflicted, and shall kill you: and ye shall be hated of all nations for my name's sake.

NOTE PAGE

NOTE PAGE

NOTE PAGE

NOTE PAGE

NOTE PAGE

Chapter 3

Bullying in WWII

There were over 1000 concentration camps but they all didn't start as death camps. First they were to hold prisoners of war. Then in the 1940s they created the crematoria and slaughter of innocent people not just Jews although they took the biggest hit. There where the most horrific atrocities known to mankind in those camps. There were so many concentration camps I will be discussing the most notorious places of cruelty (bullying) done to non believers in the Nazi regime. As stated in the acknowledgements one of my high school friend's dad was incarcerated in Dresden. He had to ride the boxcars and they were piled in 1200 in each boxcar leaving no room to sit down. They were supplied with a bucket to use the bathroom but nowhere to dump it. As a result of that Prisoners were using the bathroom and having to step in it and many diseases broke out. Some died on the way but my friend's dad had a strong will to live that he actually lived through that nightmare. Americans liberated the camp. There were so many concentration camps all throughout. Here is a map of the concentration camps from the Jewish Virtual Library: Cartography by Jen Rosenberg. Map copyright 1998, 1999, and 2000 Jen Rosenberg. Base map courtesy the U.S. Central Intelligence Agency."

I am going to cover the bullying that went on in the most notorious concentration camps.

World War II Lessons for Bullied Targets and Co-Workers What saying "no" to demonic tyranny looks like.

Lydia Greico M.A.

The Holocaust ravaged European Jews. No greater illustration of bullying and tyranny on an incomparable scale can be considered than the elimination of an entire race of people across Europe. The Nazis attempted to eradicate the Jews in every country they occupied during World War II. They called it "Eugenics" which means racial purity and America used this practice too to sterilize mentally ill and developmentally disabled persons. They didn't want to produce any disabled children either. The Germans didn't want anyone living in their country but Germans. Jews were considered "cholera bacilli", a virus and the only way to rid Germany of this virus was to exterminate it. Of course it was all for the good of Germany. Over 6 million Jews lost their lives, Adults and children as well. Over 17 million people lost their lives in WWII but the Jews took the biggest hit.

When the Nazis invaded Denmark in 1940, The Danes had an active resistance movement. It was a late-war decision to deport Danish Jews to concentration camps.

A Hero:

The German naval attache to Denmark, Georg Duckwitz, leaked the Nazi plan to begin deportation.

The People Unite:

The local population had not cooperated with the Nazis. When they learned of the plans to purge Danish Jews, they began an intense campaign to evacuate their neighbors and relatives to safety in Sweden. They were shuttled in small fishing boats carrying only about 20 people at a time. The fisherman met larger Swedish ships in the channel between the two countries.

The Simple Motivation:
The Shining Danish Example

Preben Munch-Nielson from Snekkersten, a small fishing village, who was 17 when the Jews were evacuated, is one such person. Preben was a courier in the resistance. He himself had to take refuge in Sweden in November, 1943 until his return in May, 1945 at the war's end. His account can be found at the Holocaust Museum in Washington, DC. Many Jews turned to living underground at this time. They lived in the sewers under the Ghettos, or anywhere else they could and would pay for someone to protect them and bring them food. Their children played with the rats often seeing them as the family pets. Anyone caught helping them was either shot or hung by the SS guards.

In Preben's own words ..."You can't let people in need down. You can't turn the back to people who need your help. There must be some sort of decency in a man's life and that wouldn't have been decent to turn the back. So there's no question of why or why not. You just did. That's the way you're brought up. That's the way of tradition in my country. You help of course ... could you have remained your self-respect if you knew that these people would suffer and you had said 'No, Not at my table?' No. No way. So that's not a problem—you just have to do it. And nothing else."

Tyranny Thwarted:
What does this have to do with bullying?

While in the camps Jews were beaten starved, hung, shot, and had horrible medical experiments done on them without anesthetic. They had to stand in formation for roll call days at a time and if anyone fainted or moved they were shot. The Germans were especially cruel to the Jews and bullied them every chance they got.

In October, 1943, the Gestapo began hunting Jews and treated them like animals. 7,200 of the 7,800

Danish Jews and 700 of their non-Jewish relatives were escorted to safety. Citizens who became refugees were hidden in homes near the shore and led to boats under cover of darkness. Only 51 Danish Jews perished in Nazi camps. When the Danish Jews returned home after the war, their homes were waiting for them, having been maintained by their neighbors. Life resumed. The Nazis had failed. Jews hid anywhere they couldn't be found such as in underground bunkers, the sewer systems, in old buildings, basements etc.

Finally, France and Britain had enough and the result was World War II. Initially, the camps were used to terrorize opponents of the Nazi regime. Later, (from about 1938-39 on), they provided slave labor.

From late 1941 on, *extermination camps* were set up as mass killing facilities for the 'Final Solution'.

The progression of Nazi camps:

The first concentration camps were set up in 1933. They were punishment camps set up in order to terrorize opponents of the Nazi regime. They soon became notorious for horrific brutality. In addition to genuine opponents, some other people were also sent there; for example, people who had offended local Nazi party bosses and so on. Since the purpose of these camps was to terrorize (bully) would-be opponents of the regime, information about what went on there was allowed to get out. Most of the camps established in the early months were temporary and were closed down within a few months. However, Dachau remained. The existence of these camps was **not** secret, though the precise details of what went on were 'hush-hush'. In fact, Himmler launched Dachau amid considerable publicity.

NOTE PAGE

NOTE PAGE

NOTE PAGE

NOTE PAGE

NOTE PAGE

Chapter 4

Dachau Concentration Camp

In the late 1930s a section of the SS set itself up as a business enterprise. It was at this stage that the systematic use of prisoners as slave labor on loan to business began. Established in March 1933, the Dachau concentration camp was the first regular concentration camp established by the Nazis in Germany. The camp was located on the grounds of an abandoned munitions factory near the medieval town of Dachau, about 10 miles northwest of Munich in the state of Bavaria, which is located in southern Germany. Heinrich Himmler, in his capacity as police president of Munich, officially described the camp as "the first concentration camp for political prisoners."

Dachau served as a prototype and model for other Nazi concentration camps that followed. Its basic organization, camp layout as well as the plan for the buildings were developed by Kommandant Theodor Eicke and were applied to all later camps. He had a separate secure camp near the command center, which consisted of living quarters, administration, and army camps. Eicke himself became the chief inspector for all concentration camps, responsible for molding the others according to his model.

During the first year, the camp held about 4,800 prisoners and by 1937 the number had risen to 13,260. Initially the internees consisted primarily of German Communists, Social Democrats, and other political opponents of the Nazi regime. Over time, other groups were also interned at Dachau such as Jehovah's Witnesses, Roma (Gypsies), and homosexuals, as well as "asocials" and repeat criminals. During the early years relatively few Jews were interned in Dachau and usually because they belonged to one of the above groups or had completed prison sentences after being convicted for violating the Nuremberg Laws of 1935.

In early 1937, the SS, using prisoner labor, initiated construction of a large complex of buildings on the grounds of the original camp. Prisoners were forced to do this work, starting with the destruction of the old munitions factory, under terrible conditions. The construction was officially completed in mid-August 1938 and the camp remained essentially unchanged until 1945. Dachau thus remained in operation for the entire period of the Third Reich. The area in Dachau included other SS facilities beside the concentration camp—a leader school of the economic and civil service, the medical school of the SS, etc. The KZ (Konzentrationslager) at that time was called a "protective custody camp," and occupied less than half of the area of the entire complex.

The number of Jewish prisoners at Dachau rose with the increased persecution of Jews and on November 10-11, 1938, in the aftermath of Kristallnacht (The Night of Broken Glass),Where all the synagogues and Jewish stores, bakeries places of business were either burned or destroyed by the Nazis. All the windows were broken out and the businesses were boarded up after they were ransacked. More than 10,000 Jewish men were interned in Dachau. (Most of men in this group were released after incarceration of a few weeks to a few months.)

Initially the Dachau camp was a training center for SS concentration camp guards, and the camp's organization and routine became the model for all Nazi concentration camps. The camp was divided into two sections—the camp area and the crematoria area. The camp area consisted of 32 barracks, including one for clergy imprisoned for opposing the Nazi regime and one reserved for medical experiments. The camp administration was located in the gatehouse at the main entrance. The camp area had a group of support buildings, containing the kitchen, laundry, showers, and workshops, as well as a prison block (Bunker). The courtyard between the prison and the central kitchen was used for the summary execution of prisoners. An electrified barbed-wire fence, a ditch, and a wall with seven guard towers surrounded the camp.

In 1942, the crematorium area was under construction. Crematorium and the new crematorium (Barrack X) with a gas chamber were erected. There is no credible evidence that the gas chamber in Barrack X was used to murder human beings. Instead, prisoners underwent "selection"; those who were judged too sick or weak to continue working were sent to the Hartheim "euthanasia" killing center near Linz, Austria. Several thousand Dachau prisoners were murdered at Hartheim. Further, the SS used the firing range and the gallows in the crematoria area as killing sites for prisoners. In Dachau, as in other Nazi camps, German physicians performed medical experiments on prisoners, including high-altitude experiments using a decompression chamber, malaria and tuberculosis experiments, hypothermia experiments, and experiments testing new medications. Prisoners were also forced to test methods of making seawater potable and of halting excessive bleeding. Hundreds of prisoners died or were permanently crippled as a result of these experiments. Dachau prisoners were used as forced laborers. At first, they were employed in the operation of the camp, in various construction projects, and in small handicraft industries established in the camp. Prisoners built roads, worked in gravel pits, and drained marshes. During the war, forced labor utilizing concentration camp prisoners became increasingly important to German armaments production.

Dachau also served as the central camp for Christian religious prisoners. According to records of the Roman Catholic Church, at least 3,000 religious, deacons, priests, and bishops were imprisoned there. In August 1944 a women's camp opened inside Dachau. Its first shipment of women came from Auschwitz Birkenau. Only 19 women guards served at Dachau, most of them until liberation.

In the last months of the war, the conditions at Dachau became even worse. As Allied forces advanced toward Germany, the Germans began to move prisoners in concentration camps near the front to more centrally located camps. They hoped to prevent the liberation of large numbers of prisoners. Transports from the evacuated camps arrived continuously at Dachau. After days of travel with little or no food or water, the prisoners arrived weak and exhausted, often near death. Typhus epidemics became a serious problem as a result of overcrowding, poor sanitary conditions, insufficient provisions, and the weakened state of the prisoners.

Owing to continual new transportations from the front, the camp was constantly overcrowded and the hygiene conditions were beneath human dignity. Starting from the end of 1944 up to the day of liberation, 15,000 people died, about half of all victims in KZ Dachau. Five hundred Soviet POWs were executed by firing squad.

NOTE PAGE

NOTE PAGE

NOTE PAGE

NOTE PAGE

NOTE PAGE

Chapter 5

Dachau Subcamps

In the summer and fall of 1944, to increase war production, satellite camps under the administration of Dachau were established near armaments factories throughout southern Germany. Dachau alone had more than 30 large sub-camps in which over 30,000 prisoners worked almost exclusively on armaments. Thousands of prisoners were worked and starved to death.

Following the 'Night of the Broken Glass' (9-10 November 1938) about 30,000 Jews were sent to concentration camps. By Christmas 1938, two thousand of them were dead. The main purpose was to bully them into leaving Germany.

The Nazi invasion of Poland meant that the Nazis made what they called their 'Jewish problem' much bigger. They also had to deal with the Polish resistance. Initially, Jews were herded into ghettos, which were sealed off from the surrounding areas.

In 1940 the first big concentration camp in Poland – Auschwitz – was established, initially as an exceptionally harsh forced labor camp for uncooperative Poles and members of the Polish intelligentsia and resistance.

From late 1941 onwards, extermination camps ('death camps') were set up, mainly in Poland. These were intended solely for the extermination of the Jews and homosexuals, Jehova witnesses, handicapped persons such as developmentally disabled, the elderly, and (gypsies) homeless people, and anyone who wouldn't go along with the Nazis. Most of the extermination camps were small: the aim was to kill newly arrived prisoners within 24-48 hours. This was 'assembly line' murder. The Germans used XyclonB aka cyanide pellets which they put down shoots in the gas chamber.

Several transit camps were established, which held prisoners till they could be transferred to concentration camps or extermination camps. However, a few prisoners were kept in transit camps for years.

As the Soviet Army drew close to the camps in Poland some of the inmates were transferred to camps in Germany. For example, Anne and Margot Frank were moved from Auschwitz Women's Camp to Bergen-Belsen, and Elie Wiesel was transferred from Auschwitz III (Monowitz) to Buchenwald.

In addition to the concentration camps (run by the SS), there were several labor camps run by a variety of organizations. Civilians from various Nazi-occupied territories (including Poland and Ukraine) were in effect kidnapped and sent to Germany as very cheap labor. Conditions in these camps varied but were never good. In some cases the inmates were paid in vouchers, some of which could be sent home.

Didn't these people think of what they were doing or what God wanted? NO the Germans called the Jews "Christ killers" but they were doing no better. You can't compound one sin for another.

Owing to continual new transportations from the front, the camp was constantly overcrowded and the hygiene conditions were beneath human dignity. Starting from the end of 1944 up to the day of liberation, 15,000 people died, about half of all victims in KZ Dachau. Five hundred Soviet POWs were executed by firing squad.

NOTE PAGE

NOTE PAGE

NOTE PAGE

NOTE PAGE

NOTE PAGE

Chapter 6

The Liberation of Dachau

As Allied forces advanced toward Germany, the Germans began to more prisoners from concentration camps near the front to prevent the liberation of large numbers of prisoners. Transports from the evacuated camps arrived continuously at Dachau, resulting in a dramatic deterioration of conditions. After days of travel, with little or no food or water, the prisoners arrived weak and exhausted, near death. Typhus epidemics became a serious problem due to overcrowding, poor sanitary conditions, and the weakened state of the prisoners.

On April 26, 1945, as American forces approached, there were 67,665 registered ccprisoners in Dachau and its subcamps. Of these, 43,350 were categorized as political prisoners, while 22,100 were Jews, with the remainder falling into various other categories. Starting that day, the Germans forced more than 7,000 prisoners, mostly Jews, on a death march from Dachau to Tegernsee far to the south. During the death march, the Germans shot anyone who could no longer continue; many also died of hunger, cold, or exhaustion.

On April 29, 1945 KZ Dachau was surrendered to the American Army by SS-Sturmscharführer Heinrich Wicker. A vivid description of the surrender appears in Brig. Gen. Henning Linden's official "Report on Surrender of Dachau Concentration Camp":

As we moved down along the west side of the concentration camp and approached the southwest corner, three people approached down the road under a flag of truce. We met these people about 75 yards north of the southwest entrance to the camp. These three people were a Swiss Red Cross representative and two SS troopers who said they were the camp commander and assistant camp commander and that they had come into the camp on the night of the 28th to take over from the regular camp personnel for the purpose of turning the camp over to the advancing Americans. The Swiss Red Cross representative acted as interpreter and stated that there were about 100 SS guards in the camp who had their arms stacked except for the people in the tower. He said he had given instructions that there would be no shots fired and it would take about 50 men to relieve the guards, as there were 42,000 half-crazed prisoners of war in the camp, many of them typhus infected. He asked if I were an officer of the American army, to which I replied, "Yes, I am Assistant Division Commander of the 42d Division and will accept the surrender of the camp in the name of the Rainbow Division for the American

As they neared the camp, they found more than 30 railroad cars filled with bodies brought to Dachau, all in an advanced state of decomposition. In early May 1945, American forces liberated the prisoners who had been sent on the death march.

General Dwight D. Eisenhower issued the capture of Dachau concentration camp: "Our forces liberated and mopped up the infamous concentration camp at Dachau. Approximately 32,000 prisoners were liberated; 300 SS camp guards were quickly neutralized."

A tablet at the camp commemorates the liberation of Dachau by the 42nd Infantry Division of the U.S. Seventh Army on 29 April 1945. Other claim that the first forces to enter the main camp were a battalion of the 157th Infantry Regiment of the 45th Infantry Division commanded by Felix L. Sparks. There is an on-going disagreement as to which division, the 42nd or the 45th, actually liberated Dachau because they seem to have approached by different routes and by the American

Army's definition, anyone arriving at such a camp within 48 hours was a liberator. General Patton visited the Buchenwald camp after it was liberated, but not Dachau.

The Americans found approximately 32,000 prisoners, crammed 1,600 to each of 20 barracks, which had been designed to house 250 people each. More bullying. People forced to live in unsanitary conditions, having all their belongings stolen from them including their hair, gold and silver teeth, and family heirlooms.

The number of prisoners incarcerated in Dachau between 1933 and 1945 exceeded 188,000.

The number of prisoners who died in the camp and the sub-camps between January 1940 and May 1945 was at least 28,000, to which must be added those who perished there between 1933 and the end of 1939. It is unlikely that the total number of victims who died in Dachau will ever be known.

NOTE PAGE

NOTE PAGE

NOTE PAGE

NOTE PAGE

NOTE PAGE

Chapter 7

Sobibor

The Inmates Revolt

For Sobibor Jews boarding the cattle cars had been told to carry all their valuables and enough food for three days. It turned out to be weeks and many died along the way. When they arrived at Sobibor there was music playing as if the guards were welcoming them when all they wanted were people that had a trade. All women with children, the elderly, and people who were disabled went from the train to the gas chambers through "selection" and were murdered. The only people allowed to live were the ones with trades. They wanted shoe makers, seamstresses, people with animal husbandry skills, locksmiths, Jewelers, taylors, and electricians. One had to be at least 14 years old with a trade if they were to survive. In one instance of bullying, 13 prisoners tried to escape. The SS guards told them to go through the lines of prisoners and pick a person you want to die with. At first they rebelled and a guard said "if you won't pick, I will but it will be 15 instead of 13" so they did what they were told. Then the SS guards told the people in formation that if any one of them flinched or cried or moved they too would join the prisoners that were going to die.

They were all shot by firing squad. No one made a move or showed emotion. More bullying. Every day someone was beaten to death or bullied in some way that caused death as was in the other concentration camps. The komondant then said "there will be no more escape attempts at Sobibor. Little did he know there were escape plans initiated under his nose. This would be the biggest revolt in the history of the camps. Leon Feldhendler and Alexander Percherski a Russian Jewish soldier ("Sasha") were partners in Caucasian the revolution secrecy. The idea was to kill all the guards so the prisoners could escape. All 600 prisoners were to walk out the front gate. Many of the guards were killed because the Jews themselves along with "Sasha, "who got his unit to help out. Weapons were made and artillery was stashed until the day of escape. 25 of the guards were actually killed under false pretenses of getting clothing or boots fitted. As they sat down to get fitted they were stabbed to death and hidden in whatever factory they met their demise where Jews were working. There was even an electrician who climbed the poles and cut all the lights and phone lines so the Nazis couldn't call for help. He died running for safety as well as 299 of his race This was bullying at its best. 300 prisoners made it to safety and hid either with partisans or were taken in families and given new identities. Sometimes one has to fight fire with fire. That was the case at Sobibor. The Nazis at Sobibor were especially cruel to the inmates and went out of their way to bully them and derive pleasure in doing so. Sobibor was the first camp that revolted. Sobibor was closed after this incident and the crematoria and gas chambers bombed by the Nazis to cover up all their bullying and murdering.

NOTE PAGE

NOTE PAGE

NOTE PAGE

NOTE PAGE

NOTE PAGE

NOTE PAGE

NOTE PAGE

Chapter 8

Treblinka

I have another friend who was scheduled to go to Treblinka and die the day of his Bar Mitz Vah. But as fate had it he was safe and his country told Hitler they needed their Jews to dig streets and tunnels so He was saved. God had plans for Rabbi Hiam Asa.

Treblinka wasn't a transition camp although they wanted the public eye to think that. There were no barracks, nor prisoners; just gas chambers and crematoria. People would get off the trains and go get murdered in the gas chambers then the Nazis would burn them in the crematoria. 870,000 people died in Treblinka during WWII. Treblinka was one of 6 camps erected by Germany. The others were: Berkenau, Sobibor, Auchwitz, Chelmno and Maidanek.

Auchwitz was operating in full capacity. They kidnapped Jews from the Warsaw ghetto. 5000 Jews went to

Auschwitz from the warsaw ghetto and only 2000 survived when troops liberated the camp. This was another killing factory and the gas chambers ran 24/7 and still couldn't accommodate all the death The gas chambers were nicknamed "Pathway to heaven". Each day 100 jews were chosen to haul the dead bodies to mass graves and then when they were finished burying them they too were shot. There are far too many camps to discuss in this book so I picked the worst ones with the most casualties. How could such human atrocities exist in such a technically developed country as Germany.

NOTE PAGE

NOTE PAGE

NOTE PAGE

NOTE PAGE

NOTE PAGE

Chapter 9

Auschwitcz-Birkenau

In April 1940, Rudolph Höss, who become the first commandant of Auschwitz, identified the Silesian town of Oswiecim in Poland as a possible site for a concentration camp. The function of the camp initially was planned as an intimidation to Poles to prevent resistance their to German rule and serve as a prison for those who did resist. It was also perceived as a cornerstone of the policy to re-colonize Upper Silesia, which had once been a German region, with "pure Aryans." When the plans for the camp were approved, the Nazi's changed the name of the area to Auschwitz.

On April 27th, 1940, Heinrich Himmler ordered construction of the camp.

In May 1940, Poles were evicted from the vicinity of the barracks (most of them were executed), and a work crew comprising concentration camp prisoners was sent from Sachsenhausen. 300 Jews from the large Jewish community of Oswiecim were also pressed into service. (AICE, 2013) The first transport of prisoners, almost all Polish civilians, arrived in June 1940 and the SS administration and staff was established. On March 1th, 1941, the camp population was 10,900. Quite quickly, the camp developed a reputation for torture and mass shootings. In March 1941, Himmler visited Auschwitz and commanded its enlargement to hold 30,000 prisoners. The location of the camp, practically in the center of German-occupied Europe, and its convenient transportation connections and proximity to rail lines was the main thinking behind the Nazi plan to enlarge Auschwitz and begin deporting people here from all over Europe.

At this time only the main camp, later known as Auschwitz I, had been established. Himmler ordered the construction of a second camp for 100,000 inmates on the site of the village of Brzezinka, roughly two miles from the main camp. This second camp, now known as Birkenau or Auschwitz II, was initially intended to be filled with captured Russian POWs who would provide the slave labor to build the SS "utopia" in Upper Silesia. Chemical giant I G Farben expressed an interest in utilizing this labor force, and extensive construction work began in October 1941 under terrible conditions and with massive loss of life. About 10,000 Russian POWs died in this process. The greater part of the apparatus of mass extermination was eventually built in the Birkenau camp and the majority of the victims were murdered here.

More than 40 sub-camps, exploiting the prisoners as slave laborers, were also founded, mainly as various sorts of German industrial plants and farms, between 1942 and 1944. The largest of them was called Buna (Monowitz, with ten thousand prisoners) and was opened by the camp administration in 1942 on the grounds of the Buna-Werke synthetic rubber and fuel plant, six kilometers from the Auschwitz camp. The factory was built during the war by the German cartel, and the SS supplied prisoner labor. On November 1943, the Buna sub-camp became the seat of the commandant of the third part of the camp, Auschwitz III, to which some other Auschwitz sub-camps were subordinated. The Germans isolated all the camps and sub-camps from the outside world and surrounded them with barbed wire fencing. All contact with the outside world was forbidden. However, the area administered by the commandant and patrolled by the SS camp garrison went beyond the grounds enclosed by barbed wire. It included an additional area of approximately 40 square kilometers (the so-called "Interessengebiet"—the interest zone), which lay around the Auschwitz I and Auschwitz II-Birkenau camps.

With the additions, the main camp population grew from 18,000 in December 1942 to more than 30,000 in March 1943.

In March 1942, a women's camp was established at Auschwitz with 6,000 inmates and in August it was moved to Birkenau. By January 1944, 27,000 women were living in Birkenau, in section B1a, in separated quarters.

In February 1943, a section for Gypsies was also established at Birkenau, called camp BIIe, and in September 1943 an area was set aside for Czech Jews deported from Theresienstadt, and was so-called the "Family Camp," Beginning in 1942, Auschwitz began to function in a way different than its original intent.

By late 1941, Himmler had briefed Commandant Höss about the "Final Solution" and by the following year Auschwitz-Birkenau became the center of the mass destruction of the European Jews.

Before caucasian Jewish exterminations, though, the Nazi's used the Soviet POWs at the Auschwitz camp in trials of the poison gas Zyklon-B, produced by the German company "Degesch", which was marked as the best way to kill many people at once. The POWs were gassed in underground cells in Block 11, the so called "Death Block," and following these trials, one gas chamber was setup just outside the main camp and two temporary gas chambers were opened at Birkenau.

The Nazis marked all the Jews living in Europe for total extermination, regardless of their age, sex, occupation, citizenship, or political views. They were killed for one reason, and one reason alone – because they were Jews. At Auschwitz-Birkenau, the 'Final Solution' was put to the ground in Nazi-like efficiency: When a train carrying Jewish prisoners arrived "selections" would be conducted on the railroad platform, or ramp. Newly arrived persons classified by the SS physicians as unfit for labor were sent to the gas chambers: these included the ill, the elderly, pregnant women and children. In most cases, 70-75% of each transport was sent to immediate death. These people were not entered in the camp records; that is, they received no serial numbers and were not registered, and this is why it is possible only to estimate the total number of victims.

Those deemed fit enough for slave labor were then immediately registered, tattooed with a serial number, undressed, deloused, had their body hair shaven off, showered while their clothes were disinfected with Zyklon-B gas, and entered the camp under the infamous gateway inscribed 'Arbeit Macht Frei' ("Labor will set you free"). Of approximately 2.5 million people who were deported to Auschwitz, 405,000 were given prisoner status and serial numbers. Of these, approximately 50% were Jews and 50% were Poles and other nationalities. Autumn 1943, the camp administration was reorganized following a corruption scandal. By the end of 1943, the prisoner population of Auschwitz main camp, Birkenau, Monowitz and other subcamps was over 80,000: 18,437 in the main camp, 49,114 in Birkenau, and 13,288 at Monowitz where I G Farben had its synthetic rubber plant. Up to 50,000 prisoners were scattered around 51 subcamps such as Rajsko, an experimental agricultural station, and Gleiwitz, a coal mine.

The situation in the subcamps was often even worse than in the main camps. In mid-1944, Auschwitz was designated a SS-run security area of over 40 square miles. By August 1944, the camp population reached 105,168. The last roll-call on January 18th, 1945, showed 64,000 inmates.

During its history, the prison population of Auschwitz changed composition significantly. At first, its inmates were almost entirely Polish. From April 1940 to March 1942, on about 27,000 inmates, 30 percent were Poles and 57 percent were Jews. From March 1942 to March 1943 of 162,000 inmates, 60 percent were Jews. Parallel system to the main camp in Auschwitz began to operate at the Birkenau camp by 1942. The exception, though, was that the majority of "showers" used to delouse the incoming prisoners proved to be gas chambers. At Birkenau, only about 10 percent of Jewish transports were registered, disinfected, shaven and showered in the "central sauna" before being assigned barracks as opposed to being sent directly to the death chambers.

In the spring of 1942, two provisional gas chambers at Birkenau were constructed out of peasant huts, known as the "bunkers."

The first "bunker", with two sealed rooms, operated from January 1942 to the end of that year. The second, with four air tight rooms, became redundant in the spring of 1943, but remained standing and was used again in the autumn of 1944 when extra "capacity" was needed for the murder of Hungarian Jews and the liquidation of the ghettos. The second measured about 1.134 square feet. The victims murdered in the "bunkers" were first obliged to undress in temporary wooden barracks erected nearby. Their bodies were taken out of the gas chambers and pushed to pits where they were burned in the open.

Between January 1942 and March 1943, 175,000 Jews were gassed to death here, of whom 105,000 were killed from January to March 1943.

Up to this point, though, Auschwitz-Birkenau accounted for "only" 11 percent of the victims of the 'Final Solution.' In August 1942, however, construction began on four large-scale gassing facilities. It appears from the plans that the first two gas chambers were adapted from mortuaries which, with the huge crematoria attached to them, were initially intended to cope with mortalities amongst the slave labor force in the camp, now approaching 100,000 and subject to a horrifying death rate. But from the autumn of 1942, it seems clear that the SS planners and civilian contractors were intending to build a mass-murder plant.

The twin pairs of gas chambers were numbered II and III, and IV and V. The first opened on March 31, 1943, the last on April 4, 1943. The total area of the gas chambers was 2,255 square meters; the capacity of these crematoria was 4,420 people. Those selected to die were undressed in the undressing room and then pushed into the gas chambers.

It only took about 20 minutes for all the people inside to die.

In chambers II and III, the killings took place in underground rooms, and the corpses were carried to the five ovens by an electrically operated lift. Before cremation gold teeth and any other valuables, such as rings, were removed from the corpses. In IV and V the gas chambers and ovens were on the same level, but the ovens were so poorly built and the usage was so great that they repeatedly malfunctioned and had to be abandoned. The corpses were finally burned outside, in the open, as in 1943. Jewish sonderkommandos worked the crematoria under SS supervision.

Initially the new facilities were "underutilized." From April 1943 to March 1944, "only" 160,000 Jews were killed at Birkenau.

But, in May 1944, a railroad spur line was built right into the camp to accelerate and simplify the handling of the tens of thousands of Hungarian and other Jews deported in the spring and summer of 1944. From then to November 1944, when all the other death camps had been abandoned, Birkenau surpassed all previous records for mass killing. The Hungarian deportations and the liquidation of the remaining Polish ghettos, such as Lodz, resulted in the gassing of 585,000 Jews. This period made Auschwitz-Birkenau into the most notorious killing site of all time. Remarkably, there were instances of individual resistance and collective efforts at fighting back inside Auschwitz. Poles, Communists and other national groups established networks in the main camp. A few Jews escaped from Birkenau, and there were recorded assaults on Nazi guards even at the entrance to the gas chambers. The "Sonderkommando" revolt in October 1944 was the extraordinary example of physical resistance.

In October 1944, the "Sonderkommando" crew at crematoria IV revolted and destroyed the crematoria. It was never used again. In November of 1944, in the face of the approaching allied Red Army, Himmler ordered gassings to stop and for a "clean-up" operation to be put in place in order to conceal traces of the mass murder and other crimes that they had committed. The Nazi's destroyed documents and dismantled, burned down or blew up the vast majority of buildings.

The orders for the final evacuation and liquidation of the camp were issued in mid-January 1945. The Germans left behind in the main Auschwitz camp, Birkenau and in Monowitz about 7,000 sick or incapacitated who they did not expect would live for long; the rest, approximately 58,000 people, were evacuated by foot into the depths of the Third Reich. Those prisoners capable, began forcibly marching at the moment when Soviet soldiers were liberating Cracow, some 60 kilometers from the camp. In marching columns escorted by heavily armed SS guards, these 58,000 men and women prisoners were led out of Auschwitz from January 17-21. Many prisoners lost their lives during this tragic evacuation, known as the "Death March."

When Soviet troops liberated Auschwitz on January 27, 1945, they found only the few thousand pitiful survivors who had been left behind as well as 836,525 items of women clothing, 348,820 items of men clothing, 43,525 pairs of shoes and vast numbers of toothbrushes, glasses and other personal effects. They found also 460 artificial limbs and seven tons of human hair shaved from Jews before they were murdered. The human hairs were used by the company "Alex Zink" (located in Bavaria) for confection of cloth. This company was paying the Nazi's 50 pfennig per kilo of human hair.

Of those who received numbers at Auschwitz-Birkenau, only 65,000 survived. It is estimated that only about 200,000 people who passed through the Auschwitz camps survived.

Historians and analysts estimate the number of people murdered at Auschwitz somewhere between 2.1 million to 4 million, of whom the vast majority were Jews.

NOTE PAGE

NOTE PAGE

NOTE PAGE

NOTE PAGE

NOTE PAGE

Chapter 10

Buchenwald

At Buchenwald the serial numbers were tattooed on the inmates stomach's. Buchenwald was just as gruesome as the other camps. It was also a factory of death. The inmates were made to do hard labor and were starved to death and then cremated. Along with the other concentration camps there was mass murdering done there. The doctors there did chemical experiments on children. They were injected with toxins to see what would happen. They actually had an exhibit of artwork, shrunken heads and lampshades made of human skin. They were so proud of there work they invited the public to see what had been going on there all this time. Many left sick to their stomach. The stench was overpowering with all the piles of corpses hidden away in a room where they died. The public was forced to see the atrocities that were happening there and many town folks didn't even know what was going on behind their backs. Many left vomiting or fainting to look at such abominations.

In 1939 Hitler stated "The fate of the Reich depends on me as long as I live I shall think only of victory, I shall annihilate everyone who is opposed to me. The subcamp for Buchenwald was Ravensbruck and that housed women. Same thing there, if you couldn't work you went to the gas chamber, were murdered and thrown in a ditch. They ruled by fear and sadistic acts of violence and torture. There beatings with horsewhips and gun butts. There were 164 deaths in the first month. When the war was finally over in 1945 many SS were caught and were tried at the Nuremburgh trials. ^ million Jews had lost their lives due to Hitler's bullying. Hitler Killed himself in 1945 when he realized Germany was losing the war. Many ss fled to other countries and were eventually caught and made to pay for their actions.

One reader stated "this isn't war, its bullying on a nauseatingly large scale. Another said "How are we to touch the stars when all we do is beat our fellow man". People were waking up and realized they had been duped by Hitler and he wasn't the man he portrayed himself to be. At the war's end 6 million Jews gypsies, Jehova Witnesses, homosexuals and political prisoners were murdered in Hitlers "Final solution".

NOTE PAGE

NOTE PAGE

NOTE PAGE

NOTE PAGE

# NOTE PAGE

Chapter 11

Manzanar

Yes America we did it too but not to the extent of Hitler. When the Japanese bombed Pearl Harbor The united States did it too. All the citizens of Japan that were in the United states that were citizens were taken to "internment" camps to do forced labor. Unlike Hitler they were not stripped of there citizenship. Some were even veterans of WWI. How could the internment of Japanese-Americans have occurred in "the land of the free and the home of the brave? Even before the Japanese internment many businesses were failing and the rest were frozen by the US government. Then, religious and political leaders were arrested and often put into holding facilities or relocation camps without letting their families know what had happened to them. The order to have all Japanese-Americans relocated had serious consequences for the Japanese-American community. Even children adopted by caucasian parents were removed from their homes to be relocated. Sadly, most of those relocated were American citizens by birth. Many families wound up spending three years in facilities. Most lost or had to sell their homes at a great loss and close down numerous businesses.

The War Relocation Authority (WRA) was created to set up relocation facilities. They were located in desolate, isolated places. The first camp to open was Manzanar in California. Over 10,000 people lived there at its height. The relocation centers were to be self-sufficient with their own hospitals, post offices, schools, etc. And everything was surrounded by barbed wire. Guard towers dotted the scene. The guards lived separately from the Japanese-Americans.

In Manzanar, apartments were small and ranged from 16 x 20 feet to 24 x 20 feet. Obviously, smaller families received smaller apartments. They were often built of subpar materials and with shoddy workmanship so many of the inhabitants spent some time making their new homes livable. Further, because of its location, the camp was subject to dust storms and extreme temperatures.

At the close of WWII all the prisoners were sent home with $25.00 to get a bus home. Many people lost homes and businesses. Many inhabitants, however, had nowhere to go. In the end, some had to be evicted because they had not left the camps. Was this worth it to hurt our own people?

How could this happen on our own soil America? How could this happen in the land of the free and the home of the brave? At the end of WWII the camp was closed and still today sits a memorial.

In 1988, President Ronald Reagan signed the Civil Liberties Act that provided redress for Japanese-Americans. Each living survivor was paid $20,000 for the forced incarceration. In 1989, President Bush issued a formal apology.

In essence we had our own holocaust with the Japanese Americans. Hitler did the same thing when he stripped the Jews of their German citizenship. This is bullying on a national and international scale. So what does all this have to do with bullying??? Read on. I promise you will know by the end of the book.

Accepting Jesus As Lord, Savior, And God "For if you confess with your lips that Jesus is Lord, and believe in your heart that God raised Him from the dead, you will be saved."

—Romans 10:9

The tongue of the wise dispenses knowledge, but the mouths of fools pour out folly. A gentle tongue is a tree of life.

—Prov.15:2:4

NOTE PAGE

NOTE PAGE

NOTE PAGE

NOTE PAGE

NOTE PAGE

Chapter 12

Why did I write about bullying first then do the concentration camps second?

Simple, To compare the bullying of today to the bullying to yesterday. It's just as bad. We have churches burned all the time, what did they do in krystalnacht? People die in churches all the time. They can't even leave a church open anymore because of vandals, or hate crimes. All these incidences are called mini holocausts and that is not to defame those who lost family and friends in the holocaust. In this chapter I will talk about all the comparisons of the holocaust to the incidents of today and provide scriptural support for them. Bullies more often than not kill their victims just as the Nazis killed the Jews. They do cruel things to their victims as well just as the Nazis did in the holocaust.

Why do you think all these disasters are falling upon us? Hurricane Sandy, Hurricane Katrina, tornadoes in places there haven't been any for years. Earthquakes are a common thing now to be in and have the experience. California isn't the only lucky state to have earthquakes. I was visiting my sister in Virginia a few years back and there was a 4.8. That was the talk of the town for the 2 weeks I was there. Maybe Jesus wants our attention and is calling his flock to pay more attention to his ways and his works. I remember one year there was a hurricane in Florida and someone placed a sign above their dwelling that was ruined and it said " ok Jesus we get it" those people probably straightened out in a hurry. Jesus wants all of us to repent and love him.

Columbine High School Kids went on a shooting spree killing their peers that loved Jesus. Sounds like the holocaust to me. Jews died because of who they were and what they believed. Now the same thing is happening here in America; In the land of the free and the home of the brave. Don't we get it? Jesus wants us to be one in him. He wants all religions to join hands and celebrate him together as one. Catholic means universal so he wants all of us who practice in his name as one group. But, readers do we really " get it"? Why today is the world like it is? Why is there terrorism? Why is there so much hate? Why do we have to fear for our lives? We are all being bullied in one way or another and yet we are allowing it to happen.

Why is this? Is it some kind of inborn fear we have? No, it's because we live in a Godless society. Sure there are many Christians, but not enough obviously. Why can't we all turn to God before it is too late? We have free will. Unlike animals we can make choices; the right choices. So why aren't we doing that? Why do we have to be victims of ourselves? Victims always be true to yourselves. Don't let anyone force you to be something that in their eyes is good. You only have to please God and of course your parents and teachers or your work supervisors. Haters will always be out there to hurt some group or another. Stay the course. Fight back with education; self defense classes, whatever it takes. Pray for your enemy. The devil loves what is happening today. Its him that is wreaking havoc on the world. Go to a friend and tell them your feelings if you are being victimized by bullies. If you kill yourself you are giving them the satisfaction they want. Tell your parents or your pastor. Tell everyone you know because the more people who know the more protection and guidance you will have. Remember DON'T TAP OUT. Don't let them win.

NOTE PAGE

NOTE PAGE

NOTE PAGE

NOTE PAGE

NOTE PAGE

Chapter 13

A Comparison and A Contrast
Bullies VS. Nazis

Bullies Behavior	Nazi's Behavior
Makes own rules and can change them at any time	Makes own rules and can change them at any time
Take victims out of comfort zone	Take victims out of comfort zone ie ghettos and concentration camps
Force victims to "like them"	Force victims to "like them"
Physically assault their victims.	Physically assault their victims
Example: bully beats up victim.	Nazi's beat the jews and other inmates at camps and ghettos
Bullies feel their victims are beneath them and try to force their thoughts on victims.	Hitler started WWII to bully the Jews out of Germany because he felt they were beneath him.

Break laws as it suits them.	Hitler broke the laws of humanity.
Bullies use their victims as scapegoats.	Nazis made their victims scapegoats.
Mental Manipulation.	Nazi's manipulated the Jews into thinking they were going to take a shower but in reality there were going to be gassed.
Bullies torture, beat up and harm their victims.	Nazi's tortured, beat up and harmed their victims.
Puts fear into their victims.	Put fear into their victims.
Victims obey the bully because of fear of retaliation.	People in the concentration camps and ghettos obeyed the rules the Nazi's put forth because of fear of harm and going to the gasses.
Bullies firmly rule their territory to maintain internal and external strength within the gang.	Nazi's ruled by force and fear using weaponry, gas chambers and crematoria.
Bullies recruit others to help them bully their victims.	Hitler hired thousands of Nazi's to fulfill his task.
Bullies are strict and arrogant.	Nazi's were strict and arrogant.

Justice Robert H. Jackson stated "The wrongs we seek to condemn and punish have been so calculated, so malignant, and devastating that civilization cannot tolerate their being ignored because it cannot survive their being repeated".

A Prayer for Our Country

O Most Blessed Virgin Mary, Mother of Mercy, at this most critical time, we entrust the United States of America to your loving care.

Most Holy Mother, we beg you to reclaim this land for the glory of your Son. Overwhelmed with the burden of the sins of our nation, we cry to you from the depths of our hearts and seek refuge in your motherly protection.

Look down with mercy upon us and touch the hearts of our people. Open our minds to the great worth of human life and to the responsibilities that accompany human freedom.

Free us from the falsehoods that lead to the evil of abortion and threaten the sanctity of family life. Grant our country the wisdom to proclaim that God's law is the foundation on which this nation was founded, and that He alone is the True Source of our cherished rights to life, liberty and the pursuit of happiness.

O Merciful Mother, give us the courage to reject the culture of death and the strength to build a new Culture of Life. *Amen.*

Men of the Sacred Hearts
For additional cards, please call 586-264-8550
or email info@menofthesacredhearts.org

Final thoughts

There is now terrorism, bullying in schools, random shootings, and the hate crimes targeted at groups such as the LGBTQ community and anyone else who refuses to fit the norm that bullies set.

This behavior must stop. Bullying was the cause of WWII too. Are we looking for WWIII??? History is repeating itself. How can we make America great again when we can't even get along with ourselves? The problem and its solution doesn't just start in our Presidents lap. It also belongs to us. Start at home. Make time for your children, give them a curfew, so they aren't running around in the streets getting into trouble. Teach them morals and ethics and above all teach them about Jesus. Have a day for just the family. NO cell phones, tablets, or electronics. Just family and talk, do something together as a family. Pay attention to your kids parents; you made them now its your responsibility to make them reputable human beings and productive in society.

References

Halocaust
https://www.youtube.com/watch?v=oWKyo1R1 xo

Treblinka
https://www.youtube.com/watch?v=AXlbU5ZENy0
https://www.youtube.com/watch?v=KqLME0OP9cQ

3 teenage girls escape
https://www.youtube.com/watch?v=EHNwzg5sxOc

America gets involved
https://www.youtube.com/watch?v=aaZaoTlIx6w

Ravensbruk
https://www.youtube.com/watch?v= P4Pw17fC68
https://www.youtube.com/watch?v=aa0d2QNQbzo&oref=https%3A%2F%2Fwww.youtube.com%2Fwatch%3Fv%3Daa0d2QNQbzo&has verified=1

Dachau
https://www.youtube.com/watch?v=FMEkEGaDK6g&oref=https%3A%2F%2Fwww.youtube.com%2Fwatch%3Fv%3DFMEkEGaDK6g&has_verified=1

Liberation of Dachau
https://www.youtube.com/watch?v=sJSsilBjHd0

Auschwitz survivors tell their stories
https://www.youtube.com/watch?v=wgOiVOpCag4

Halocaust through the eyes of a child
https://www.youtube.com/watch?v=h8H alCdY8c

Auchwitz footprints in the snow
https://www.youtube.com/watch?v=afoSWxHAnrU

joseph Mengele
https://www.youtube.com/watch?v=9b4HeA4EVV8

Surviving the angel of death bullying
https://www.youtube.com/ watch?v=w4YbZzZUkKsle

Bullying
https://www.youtube.com/watch?v=oZVi4VsGi8U

Abbies story
https://www.youtube.com/watch?v=2YGjz5SV Qk

You are you
https://www.youtube.com/watch?v=l8ovOA7VhFo

Mean Girls
https://www.youtube.com/watch?v=ucPB9WhCfUM

Too Late to Appologize
https://www.youtube.com/watch?v=w7GaGFJwdd0

Stop Bullying
https://www.youtube.com/watch?v=AcZmrp-3yCs

You are not Alone
https://www.youtube.com/watch?v=tYx4CSOtsl0

Worst bullying Video ever
https://www.youtube.com/watch?v=4d-IZOBUo38

Top 10 Bullies
https://www.youtube.com/watch?v=lKjDs3z-k6s

Netflix Documentaries

http://wiki.answers.com/Q/ Why did Nazi Germany have concentration camps ret 3/19/13

Visit http://www.stopbullyingnow.com for more information about bullying, or contact Stan at stan@stopbullyingnow.com

Sources: U.S. Holocaust Memorial Museum; Wikipedia

http://www.jewishvirtuallibrary.org/jsource/Holocaust/dachau.html

http://www.youtube.com/watch?v=l8ovOA7VhFo

Friedlander, Henry. *The Origins of Nazi Genocide: From Euthanasia to the Final Solution.*

Chapel Hill: University of North Carolina Press, 1995.

*****

Aly, Götz, Peter Chroust, and Christian Pross. *Cleansing the Fatherland: Nazi Medicine and Racial Hygiene.* Baltimore, MD: Johns Hopkins University Press, 1994.

Bryant, Michael S. *Confronting the "Good Death": Nazi Euthanasia on Trial, 1945-1953.* Boulder: University Press of Colorado, 2005.

Burleigh, Michael. *Death and Deliverance: "Euthanasia" in Germany c. 1900-1945.* Cambridge: Cambridge University Press, 1994.

Gallagher, Hugh Gregory. *By Trust Betrayed: Patients, Physicians, and the License to Kill in the Third Reich.* Arlington, VA: Vandamere Press, 1995.

Davis, S Stop Bullying Now, 2013

1. ^ a b *Student Reports of Bullying*, Results From the 2001 School Crime Supplement to the National Crime Victimization Survey, US National Center for Education Statistics

2. ^ Cambridgeshire.gov.uk

3. ^ (U.S. Dept. of Justice, Fact Sheet#FS-200127)

4. ^ Harassment, Discrimination and Bullying Policy – University of Manchester

5. ^ At least 15 states have passed laws addressing bullying among school children. Google Search

6. ^ Bennett, Elizabeth *Peer Abuse Know More: Bullying From a Psychological Perspective* (2006)

7. ^ "The Balance of Power in Europe (1871-1914)". 2010. Retrieved 2010-10-30. Description of how an imbalance of power in Europe precipitated WWI.

8. ^ "The Economic Consequences of the Peace". 2005. Retrieved 2010-10-30. Describes likely connection

between imbalanced Treaty of Versailles and World War II

9. ^ <u>Etymology of bully</u>

10. ^ *a b* Whitted, K.S. & Dupper, D.R. (2005). Best Practices for Preventing or Reducing Bullying in Schools. *Children and Schools*, Vol. 27, No. 3, July 2005, pp. 167-175(9).

11. ^ <u>Complete Newgate Calendar</u> Tarlton Law Library The University of Texas School of Law

12. ^ <u>George Alexander Wood and Alexander Wellesley Leith</u> The Complete Newgate Calendar Volume V, Tarlton Law Library The University of Texas School of Law

13. ^ Zwerdling, Alex (1987) <u>Virginia Woolf and the Real World</u> p.263

14. ^ Pawlowski, Merry M. (2001) *Virginia Woolf and fascism: resisting the dictators' seduction* p.104

15. ^ *a b* Besag, V. E. (1989) Bullies and Victims in Schools. Milton Keynes, England: Open University Press

16. ^ Olweus, D., <u>Olweus.org</u>

17. ^ Carey, T.A. (2003) Improving the success of anti-bullying intervention programs: A tool for matching programs with purposes. International Journal of Reality Therapy, 23(2), 16-23

18. ^ Crothers, L. M. & Levinson, E. M. (2004, Fall). Assessment of Bullying: A review of methods and instruments. Journal of Counseling & Development, 82(4), 496-503.

19. ^ a b Ross, P. N. (1998). Arresting violence: A resource guide for schools and their communities. Toronto: Ontario Public School Teachers' Federation.

20. ^ Juvonen (2003) *Bullying Among Young Adolescents: The Strong, the Weak and the Troubled* in *Pediatrics*, December 2003, "The benefits of bullying". 2004. Retrieved 2011-09-03.

21. ^ "Bullies are healthiest pupils". *BBC News*. 1999-12-14. Retrieved 2011-09-03.

22. ^ "Child Development Academician says Bullying is beneficial to Kids". 2009. Retrieved 2011-09-03.

23. ^ Hamilton, Fiona. *The Times* (London). http://www.timesonline.co.uk/tol/news/uk/education/article7133986.ece.

24. ^ "Overview of State Anti-Bullying Legislation and Other Related Laws", journalistsresource.org.

25. ^ *Anti-Bullying Center* Trinity College, Dublin.

26. ^ Williams, K. D., Forgás, J. P. & von Hippel, W. (Eds.) (2005). *The Social Outcast: Ostracism, Social Exclusion, Rejection, & Bullying.* Psychology Press: New York, NY.

27. ^ Kim YS, Leventhal B; Leventhal (2008). "Bullying and suicide. A review". *International Journal of Adolescent Medicine and Health* **20** (2): 133-54. doi:10.1515/ IJAMH.2008.20.2.133. PMID 18714552.

28. ^ *The Harassed Worker*, Brodsky, C. (1976), D.C. Heath and Company, Lexington, Massachusetts.

29. ^ *Petty tyranny in organizations*, Ashforth, Blake, Human Relations, Vol. 47, No. 7, 755-778 (1994)

30. ^ *Matonismo es la principal forma de violencia en el 'cole'*, in *La Nación*, 16/05/2010, quotation:

31. ^ *Bullying and emotional abuse in the workplace. International perspectives in research and practice*, Einarsen, S., Hoel, H., Zapf, D., & Cooper, C. L. (Eds.)(2003), Taylor & Francis, London.

32. ^ Batsche, George M.; Knoff, Howard M. (1994). "Bullies and their victims: Understanding a pervasive problem in the schools". *School Psychology Review* **23** (2):165-175.

33. ^ Patterson G (December 2005). "The bully as victim?". *Paediatric Nursing* **17** (10):27-30. PMID 16372706.

34. ^ Kumpulainen K (2008). "Psychiatric conditions associated with bullying". *International Journal of Adolescent Medicine and Health* **20** (2): 121-

35. ^ Hazlerr, R. J.; Carney, J. V.; Green, S.; Powell, R.; Jolly, L. S. (1997). "Areas of Expert Agreement on Identification of School Bullies and Victims". *School Psychology International* **18**: 5.

36. ^ Craig, W.M. (1998). "The relationship among bullying, victimization, depression, anxiety, and aggression in elementary school children". *Personality and Individual Differences* **24** (1): 123-130. doi:10.1016/ S0191-8869(97)00145-1.

37. ^ Ferguson, Christopher J. (2011). "Video Games and Youth Violence: A Prospective Analysis in Adolescents.". *Journal of Youth and Adolescence* **40** (4).

38. ^ "Bullies, Victims, and Bystanders–Bystanders". 2010. Retrieved 2010-11-17. Description of typical attitudes of bystanders to bullying.

39. ^ "New Tactics To Tackle Bystander's Role In Bullying". 2010. Retrieved 2010-11-17. Science Daily website reviews effectiveness of several bullying-bystander awareness programs.

40. ^ "Petty Tyrant: Text intro: NPR documentary (see audio link below)". 2010. Retrieved 2010-11-17.

41. ^ "Petty Tyrant: Audio link". 2010. Retrieved 2010-11-17. Audio link to 'Petty Tyrant' NPR documentary.

42. ^ "Pasco County Students Making Friends and Stopping Bullying". 2010. Retrieved 2010-11-27.

43. ^ "Program Helps Students Combat Bullying". 2010. Retrieved 2010-11-27

44. ^ E. D. Nelson and R. D. Lambert, "Sticks, Stones and Semantics: The Ivory Tower," Qualitative Sociology, 2001: 83-106

45. ^ "Problem Solving to Prevent Bullying". 2010. Retrieved 2010-10-31

46. ^ "Bullying and Hazing: What Can We Do About These Problems?". 2010. Retrieved 2010-11-27.

47. ^ "Safe schools: Breaking the cycle of violence". 2010. Retrieved 2010-11-27. Discussion of proactive anti-bullying school plans by certified mediator, Meadow Clark.

48. ^ "Jay Banks NBC TV-10 "STAMP Out Bullying"". 2010. Retrieved 2010-10-31. Youtube video of NBC report on Jay Banks' anti-bullying program, advising targets to "project self-confidence".

49. ^ "Jay Banks Productions Youtube Homepage". 2010. Retrieved 2010-10-31. Compilation of anti-bullying videos by anti-bullying expert, Jay Banks

50. ^ Ellen deLara; Garbarino, James (2003). *And Words Can Hurt Forever: How to Protect Adolescents from Bullying, Harassment, and Emotional Violence*. New York: Free Press. ISBN 0-7432-2899-5. [page needed]

51. ^ Whitted, K.S. (2005). *Student reports of physical and psychological maltreatment in schools: An under-explored aspect of student victimization in schools*. University of Tennessee.

52. ^ Whitted, K. S.; Dupper, D. R. (2007). "Do Teachers Bully Students?: Findings From a Survey of Students in an Alternative Education

Setting". *Education and Urban Society* **40** (3): 329. doi:<u>10.1177/0013124507304487</u>.

53. ^ Namie, Gary and Ruth <u>Workplace Bullying Institute Definition</u>

54. ^ Keashly L <u>Faculty Experiences with Bullying in Higher Education Causes, Consequences, and Management -Administrative Theory & Praxis Volume 32, Number 1 March 2010</u>

55. ^ Marcello C Perceptions of Workplace Bullying Among IT Professionals: A correlational analysis of workplace bullying and psychological empowerment of Workplace Bullying Among IT Professionals (2010)

56. ^ Thomson R <u>IT profession blighted by bullying</u> Computer Weekly 3 April 2008

57. ^ Richards A, Edwards SL A Nurse's Survival Guide to the Ward (2008)

58. ^ Dellasega, C Bullying Among Nurses AJN, American Journal of Nursing: January 2009 - Volume 109 -Issue 1 -p 52-58

59. ^ Bolton, José, and Stan Graeve. "No Room for Bullies: from the Classroom to Cyberspace." Boys Town, Neb.: Boys Town, 2005.

60. ^ www.schoolbullyingcouncil.com

61. ^ Quarmby, Katharine. "Scapegoat: Why we are failing disabled people." *Portobello*, 2011.

62. Jean M. Callaghan and Franz Kernic 2003 Armed Forces and International Security: Global Trends and Issues, Lit Verlag, Munster. ^ Karim, Nadiya (2010-01-15). "Bullying in Universities: It exists". *The Independent* (London). Retrieved 2011-05-28. Discussion of bullying problem in universities and beyond.

http://www.bullyingstatistics.org/content/bullying-teachers.html Retrieved Sept. 9, 2013

Collins, Donald E. *Native American Aliens: Disloyalty and the Renunciation of Citizenship by Japanese Americans During World War II*. Westport, CN: Greenwood Press, 1985. [On "disloyals" at Tule Lake, renunciation of citizenship, and the ordeal o f seeking its restoration.]

Commission on Wartime Relocation and Internment of Civilians. *Personal Justice Denied: Report of the Commission on wartime Relocation and Internment of Civilians*. 2 Vols. Washington, DC: Government Printing Office, 1982. [Report of the Congressi onal commission summarizes the

Japanese American World War II experience; the second volume consists of the commission's recommendations for reparations.]

Conrat, Maisie, and Richard Conrat. *Executive Order 9066: The Internment of 110,000 Japanese Americans.* Cambridge, MA: Massachusetts Institute of Technology Press, 1972. Los Angeles: UCLA Asian American Studies Center, 1992. [Photographic exhibit catalog of the removal and detention of Japanese Americans.1

Daniels, Roger. *Prisoners Without Trial: Japanese Americans in World War II.* New York: Hill and Wang, 1993. [Short (114 pages of text) overview of the Japanese American World War II experience including a section on the redress movement. Also includes photographs and a section on recommended reading.]

Sandra C. Taylor, and Harry H. L. Kitano. *Japanese Americans: From Relocation to Redress.* Salt Lake City: University of Utah Press, 1986. Revised Edition. Seattle: University of Washington Press, 1991. Drinnon

Richard. *Keeper of Concentration Camps: Dillon S. Myer and American Racism.* Berkeley: University of California

Press, 1987. [Biography of WRA (and later Bureau of Indian Affairs) director Myer.]

Gardiner, C. Harvey. *Pawns in a Triangle of Hate: The Peruvian Japanese and the United States.* Seattle: University of Washington Press, 1981.

Ichioka, Yuji, and ed. "Views from Within: The Japanese American Evacuation and Resettlement Study." Los Angeles: UCLA Asian American Studies Center, 198

Irons, Peter. *Justice at War: The Story of the Japanese American Internment Cases.* New York: Oxford University Press, 1983.

James, Thomas. *Exile Within: The Schooling of Japanese Americans, 1942-1945.* Cambridge: Harvard University Press, 1987.

Kikuchi, Charles. *The Kikuchi Diary: Chronicle from an American Concentration Camp.* John Modell, ed. and introd. Urbana: University of Illinois Press, 1973. Nelson, Douglas W. *Heart Mountain: The History of an American Concentration Camp.* Madison, WI: The State Historical Society of Wisconsin, 1976.

Okihiro, Gary Y. *Cane Fires: The Anti-Japanese Movement in Hawaii, 1865-1945*. Philadelphia: Temple University Press, 1991. [Includes several chapters on Hawaii Japanese Americans interned during the war.]

Okubo, Mine. *Citizen 13660*. New York: Columbia University Press, 1946. New York: AMS Press, 1966. New preface by author. New York: Arno Press, 1978. Seattle: University of Washington Press, 1983. [Book of line drawings and text based on the author's experiences at Tanforan Assembly Center and Topaz.]

Tateishi, John. *And Justice For All: An Oral History of the Japanese American Detention Camps*. New York: Random House, 1984. [Transcribed oral histories with thirty Japanese Americans" 'focusing on their camp experiences.]

Taylor, Sandra C. *Jewel of the Desert: Japanese American Internment at Topaz*. Berkeley: Press, 1993. [Study of Topaz.]

_____. *Desert Exile: The Uprooting of a Japanese American Family*. Seattle: University of Washington Press, 1982. [Autobiographical account of removal and detention at Topaz, Utah by well-known author of children's books.]

The View from Within: Japanese American Art from the Internment Camps, 1942-1945. Los Angeles: Japanese American National Museum, UCLA Wright Art Gallery, and UCLA Asian American Studies Center, 1992. [Catalog from an exhibit of art produced by Japanese Americans while in the camps.]

Weglyn, Michi. *Years of Infamy: The Untold Story of Americas Concentration Camps.* New York: William Morrow & Co., 1976. [Overview of the removal and detention of Japanese Americans during World War II.]

http://www.adolfhitler.dk/new page 8.htm retrieved March, 10,2015

https://www.bing.com/videos/search?q=similar+behaviors+between+bullies+and+nazis&view=detail&mid=03CE2F32E520819C575F03CE2F32E520819C575F&FORM=VIRE2

Retrieved July, 22, 2016

Homepage Jewish Virtual Library –Homepage

Retrieved June, 2013

List of Nazi concentration camps –Wikipedia, the free encyclopedia Retrieved June, 2013

<u>Manzanar National Historic Site</u> –<u>Manzanar National Historic Site</u> <u>For Teachers</u> –<u>Manzanar National Historic Site</u> <u>Manzanar –Wikipedia, the free encyclopedia Category:Jewish history–Wikipedia, the free encyclopedia</u> Retrieved June, 2013

<u>Stop Bullying Now! Information And Parent/ Teacher Resources To Stop Bullies And School Violence</u> Retrieved May, 2014

ABCNEWS.com Stopping Kids From Bullying <u>Others</u> Retrieved January, 2016

Documentaries obtained from NETFLIX

    The Boy With the Striped Pajamas
    Empty Boxcars
    Shindler's List
    Out of the Ashes
    The Devil's Arithmetic
    I Have Never Forgotten You
    Blessed is the Match-The Life of Hannah Senesh
    Nazi's: A warning From History
    Holocaust The Liberation of Auschwitz
    The Liberation of Madjanek
    Au Revoir Les Enfants

Playing for Time

Fateless

Rosanstrasse

Into the arms of a Stranger

Amen

The Grey Zone

Life is Beautiful

The Pianist

Conspiracy

I'm Still Here

The Hiding Place

The Nazi's Officers Wife

Secrets From the Dead-Escape From Auschwitz

Death in The Bunker: Time Story of Hitler

Hitler in Color

Ravensbruck and Buchenwald

Divided We Fall

My Knees Were Jumping: Remembering Kindertransport

The Reisch Underground

The Unknown Soldier

A Film Unfinished

Hitler's Children

No Place on Earth

Lydia Greico M.A.

Documentaries From YouTube

Empty Boxcars, A documentary by Ed Gaffney. Chapters 1-6
https://www.youtube.com/watch?v=1rH-1DccRqA

holocaust
https://www.youtube.com/watch?v=oWKyo1R1xo

https://www.youtube.com/watch?v=AXlbU5ZENy0

treblinka
https://www.youtube.com/watch?v=KqLME0OP9cQ

3 teenage girls escape
https://www.youtube.com/watch?v=EHNwzg5sxOc

America gets involved
https://www.youtube.com/watch?v=aaZaoTlIx6w

Ravensbruk
https://www.youtube.com/watch?v= P4Pw17fC68
https://www.youtube.com/watch?v=aa0d2QNQbzo&oref=https%3A%2F%2Fwww.youtube.com%2Fwatch%3Fv%3Daa0d2QNQbzo&has verified=1

Dachau
https://www.youtube.com/watch?v=FMEkEGaDK6g&oref=https%3A%2F%2F

www.youtube.com%2Fwatch%3Fv%3DFMEkE
GaDK6g&has verified=1

Liberation of Dachau
https://www.youtube.com/watch?v=sJSsilBjHd0

Auschwitz survivors tell their stories
https://www.youtube.com/watch?v=wgOiVOpCag4

Holocaust through the eyes of a child
https://www.youtube.com/watch?v=h8H alCdY8c

Auchwitz footprints in the snow
https://www.youtube.com/ watch?v=afoSWxHAnrU

joseph Mengele
https://www.youtube.com/watch?v=9b4HeA4EVV8

Surviving the angel of death
https://www.youtube.com/ watch?v=w4YbZzZUkKsle

bullying
https://www.youtube.com/watch?v=oZVi4VsGi8U

bullying

Abbies story
https://www.youtube.com/watch?v=2YGjz5SV Qk

You are you
https://www.youtube.com/watch?v=l8ovOA7VhFo

Mean Girls
https://www.youtube.com/watch?v=ucPB9WhCfUM

Too Late to Appologize
https://www.youtube.com/watch?v=w7GaGFJwdd0

Stop Bullying
https://www.youtube.com/watch?v=AcZmrp-3yCs

You are not Alone
https://www.youtube.com/watch?v=tYx4CSOtsl0

Worst bullying Video ever
https://www.youtube.com/watch?v=4d-IZOBUo38

Top 10 Bullies
https://www.youtube.com/watch?v=lKjDs3z-k6s

Retrieved April 25, 2017
http://search.aol.com/aol/search?q=a+list+of+all+the+concentration+camps+in+europe&sit=tb50-ff-aimright-chromesbox-en-us

Hats are 16.00 and Tshirts are 15.00 and come in all sizes and colors. Shipping and handling is 5.00. They are available by the autor of this book at skater.pt1@verizon.net and thetdolife@gmail.com

www.ingramcontent.com/pod-product-compliance
Lightning Source LLC
LaVergne TN
LVHW091047100526
838202LV00077B/3063